D0289009

INTRODUCTION

Hello kids,

I'm sure you all know what a YoYo is. I bet you do! It's hard to find a kid who does not know what a YoYo is. However, do you know there are many ways to enjoy and bring the best out of a YoYo? Perhaps, you know just a few basic tricks. I've good news for you. The fun just got bigger! In this book, you'll learn 100 amazing YoYo tricks. This book was put together with you and your friends in mind so you can have fun with the YoYo and learn while at it. Happy Reading!

Bonus!

Would you like to have an exclusive article **eBook** that has **15 Top Quality Working on Crafts for Kids**?

http://bit.ly/2qWfaKT

Thank you for reading this book! I would like to give you full access to an exclusive article eBook that has **15 Top Quality Working on Crafts for Kids.** If you are someone who is interested in saving lots

of money, then type in the website on your browser for **FREE** access!

Contents

FOR BEGINNERS

1. Gravity pull yo-yo trick: This is the classic up and down yo-yo trick. The very beginning for learners

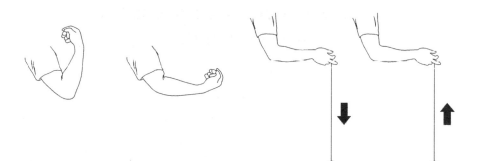

2. The throwdown yo-yo trick:
Here is a simple trick that would come in handy as you go deeper.

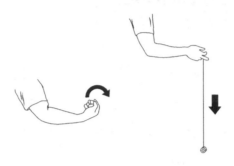

3. The sleeper yo-yo trick: This is an important skill that is used in many other yo-yo tricks.

4. The forward pass yo-yo trick:

You should learn to throw and catch, that's the core of this trick

5. Walk the dog yo-yo trick:
Raise on leg up and spin on the ground. This trick is cool but needs practice.

6. Around the world yo-yo trick:
here you spin and swing your yo-yo in a complete 360-degree arc.

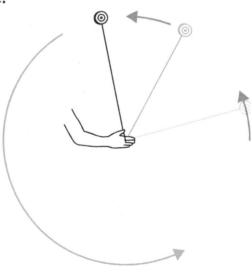

7. **Around the corner Yo-yo trick:** You take your yo-yo and give it a quick spin over your arm to the ground.

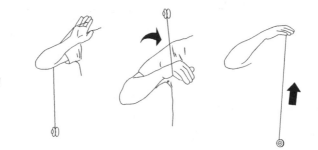

8. **Skin the cat yo-yo trick:** take your yo-yo skill to the next level by trying this one.

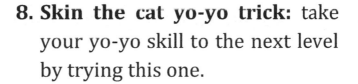

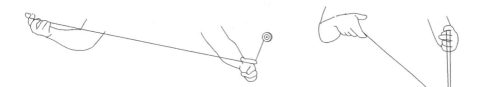

9. Rock the baby: Here is the most entertaining and popular yo-yo trick of all time. Try it during family times and when you hang out with friends

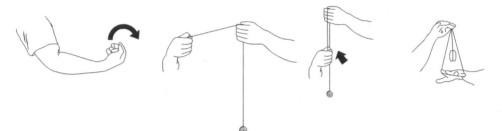

10.   Three- leaf Clover: Here is a significant yo-yo trick. You can make a wish and send it out

11. The breakaway yo-yo trick: This defies the laws of gravity that makes your yo-yo hang in the air.

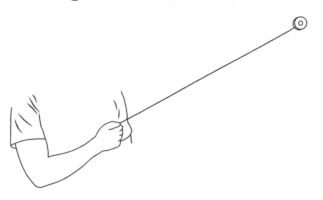

12. Reverse sleeper yo-yo trick: use a backspin and flick a sleeper

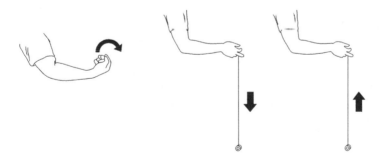

13. Walk the cat yo-yo trick:
Crack people up and entertain with this trick.

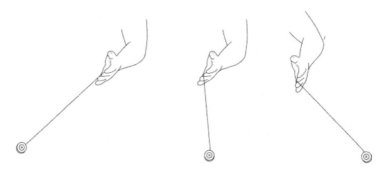

14. Pinwheel yo-yo trick:
Thrill everyone with the most beautiful yo-yo trick.

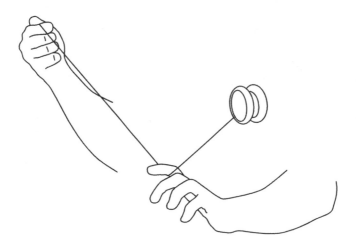

15.   Sleeping beauty yo-yo
trick: Make a classic yo-yo trick
on its side in the mid-air.

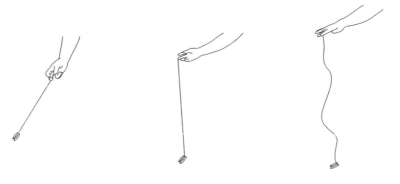

16.   Loop the loop yo-yo trick:

This trick is quite challenging, but you will get it with practice.

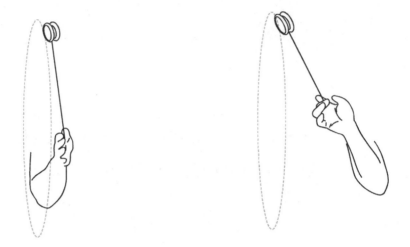

17.   Hop the fence yo-yo trick:

Once you master the loop the loop trick, this will be a work over.

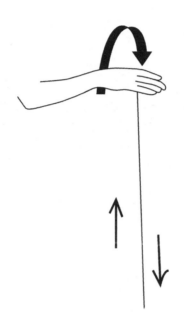

18. Walk the tightrope yo-yo

trick: Learn to walk your yo-yo along its own string.

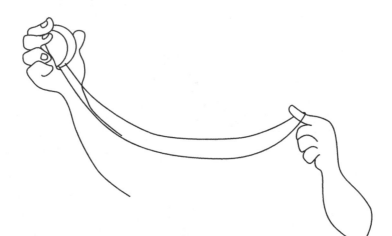

19. Outside loops yo-yo trick:

This is a new variation on the Loop the loop trick.

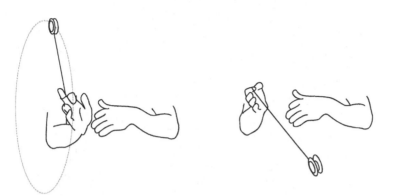

20. Double Stall: Once you get a hold of the loop the loop trick, this will be easy.

21. Walk the tight rope yo-yo trick:

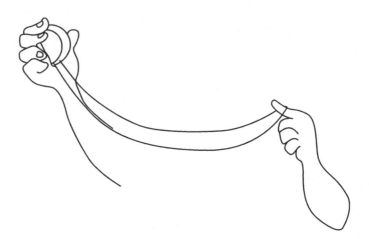

22.   Outside Loops Yo-Yo trick

Learn how to carry out a different variation on the loop. This trick is a new addition to your list of new tricks.

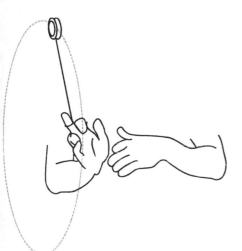
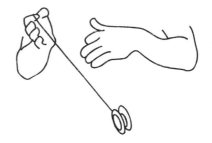

23.   Dog bite yo-yo trick

The key to doing this trick is to act surprised when the dog bites you. Don't start giggling before it happens!

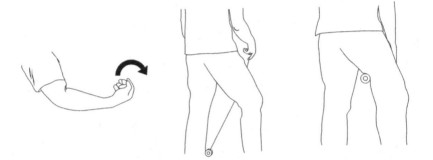

24.   Jump the Dog through the hoop yo-yo trick

This variation on Walk the Dog will make you look like a yo-yo champion.

25.   Motorcycle yo-yo trick

Get everyone's motor running with this yo-yo trick. Sound effects not included.

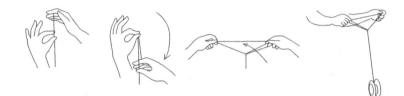

26.   Monkey climb the tree yo-yo trick

Here, the yo-yo goes against gravity and vertically climb the string. Follow the yo-yo as it moves up to improve the visual effect.

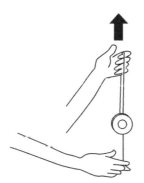 

27. Slurp the spaghetti yo-yo trick

This trick demands that you overact and do it right. When done right, the result is more like you are eating spaghetti in the real sense.

28.   Hidemassa yoyo trick:

This trick is pretty simple. Simply start with your breakaway trick, then pop up the yoyo and swing the string beneath it.

29.   Slack trapeze yoyo trick -
This trick status with the
trapezo trick. Then hop the yoyo
right back.

30.   **Magic drop and Shockwave yoyo trick** - Start with the trapeze trick and wrap the string around your thumb. Your aim is to make the string go round your thumb and also hold the string on the end of your first finger.

31. **Seasick yoyo trick** - This trick starts with the split bottom mount, then bounce your yoyo back and forth above your head.

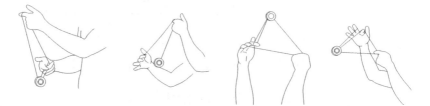

32. **Grind introduction yoyo trick** - This trick is pretty simple. Allow the yoyo spin while touching a part of your body at the same time.

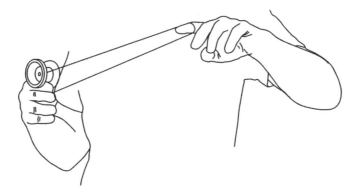

33.   Boingy boing yoyo trick -
Start with the split bottom
mount, then lay the string on
your yoyo finger over the string
on the first finger of your yoyo
hand. Ensure that the string is
straight and going up and down
perfectly.

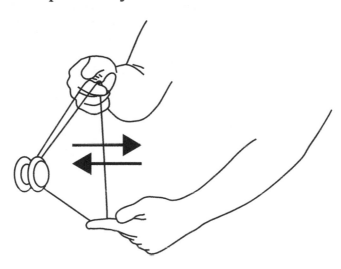

34. **Kwyjibo yoyo trick -** The trick is a series of hop. Start by hopping the yoyo from a single, then proceed to one and a half and finally, a double.

35. Gyroscopic flop yoyo trick - Simply make the yoyo rotate on an axis.

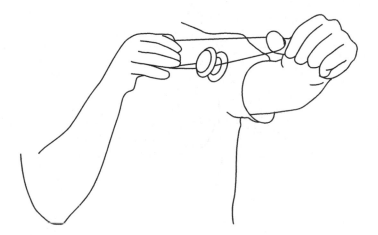

36. Two-handed loops yoyo
trick - Just as the name implies,
this trick is simply looping yoyo
with both hands.

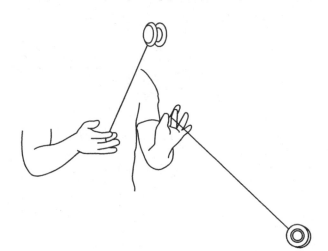

37.   Pinwheel yoyo trick -
This is a great trick to
incorporate into other tricks.
Ensure the place at which your
yoyo is spinning is the same as
the starting point.

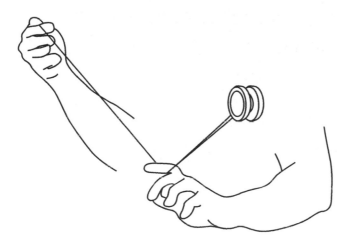

38. **Side mount corrections yoyo trick** - Chances are you are going to miss when learning the sidemount tricks. Should you miss, simply pinch the string with your thumb, bend your finger and place then underneath. Then use the finger to toss your yoyo back on the string.

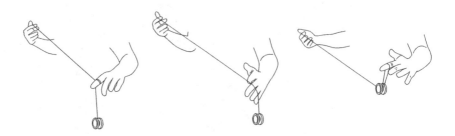

39. Man on the flying trapeze

yoyo trick - This trick is done alongside the string trick.

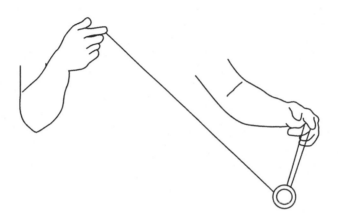

40.   String trick terminology -

The trick entails the yoyo landing on the string. So it's best to use a wider yoyo.

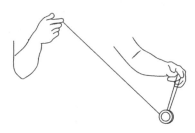 

41. **Flips yoyo trick -** This trick is the opposite of the loop trick. The flip trick is done with a wider yoyo.

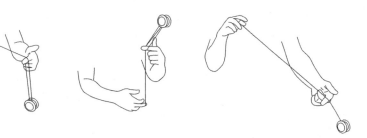

42. **Looping introduction yoyo trick -** This trick starts with a forward toss. Once you have gotten that, the yoyo gets back to the starting point. Then, bend your wrist backward to throw the yoyo again.

43.   All around yoyo trick -
Just as the name implies, the
yoyo moves all around. The trick
is a combination of both the
basic loop and the forward toss.

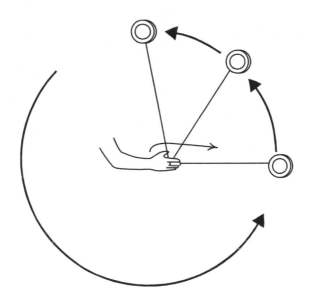

**44.   Wind the string yoyo
trick** - Adjust your yoyo
properly to match with your
height. Then, wind your yoyo up
the string. Ensure that the yoyo
is spinning.

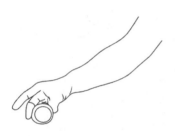

45. **Eli hops yoyo trick - This**
trick is similar to man on the
flying trapeze trick. The trick is
simple. Simply pop the yoyo off
and catch it right back. To be
successful with this trick, ensure
your opposite finger is in
contact with the string.

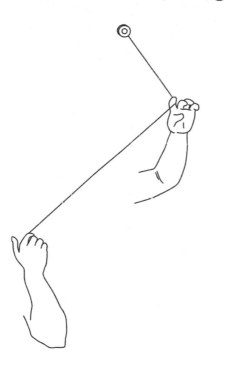

46.   Eiffel Tower yoyo trick -
This is an easy and a classic trick
that is sure to leave great
impression on your family and
friends. It's more like a picture
trick, you only need to leave the
yoyo down the string without
having to spin it.

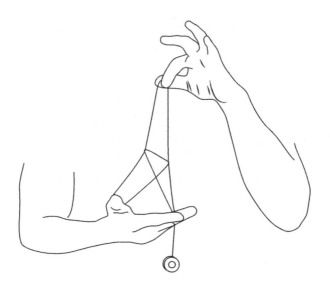

47.   Forward toss yoyo trick -
This is the first trick to learn if
you are just starting out. Simply
learn how to throw your yoyo
forward.

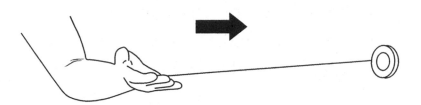

48. **Side mount flip yoyo trick** - To be successful with this trick, you need to master reverse flips and forward on the front mount. Once you have learnt this, doing them on the side isn't difficult. You only need to keep in mind that the side mount is done in reverse.

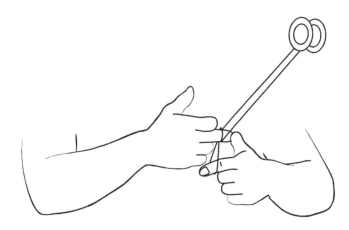

49.   Barrel rolls yoyo trick -

The barrel rolls can be done on both side and front mount, just like the reverse flips and forward flips.

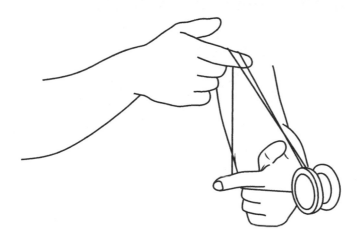

50. Slip the atom yoyo trick -

This trick starts with the split bottom mount. Then, pass your opposite hand beneath the yoyo and hold the yoyo on the string.

51. Thread the needle yo-yo trick

A variation on Monkey Climb the Tree, this yo-yo trick takes a very steady hand.

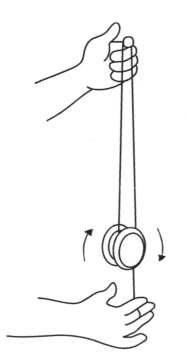

52.   Corral gate yo-yo trick

Practice making the Corral Gate with a non-spinning yo-yo before you try this trick at full speed.

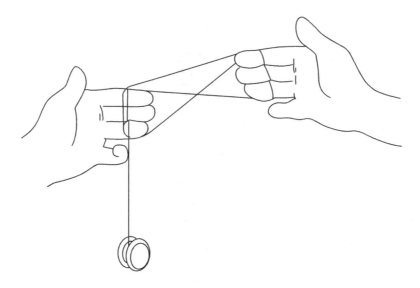

53.   Eiffel tower yo-yo trick

You don't need to take your friends&
family to France to show them the
Eiffel Tower. You can make magic
with your YoYo.

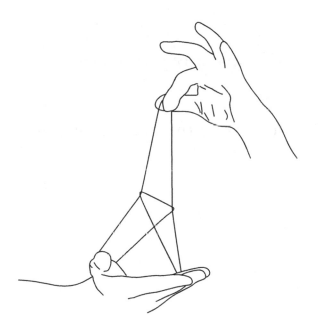

PROFESSIONAL YOYO TRICKS

Here, you will learn yo-yo tricks that will make you look like a professional.

54.   Texas star yo-yo trick

Do you know that you can shape your yo-yo string into a star in honor of the great state of Texas. Supercool right?

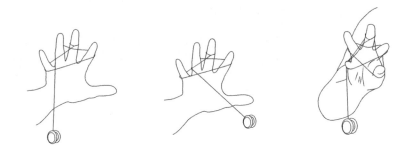

55. One-Handed star yo-yo trick

You can make a star out of your yo-yo string with just one hand. It's amazong right!

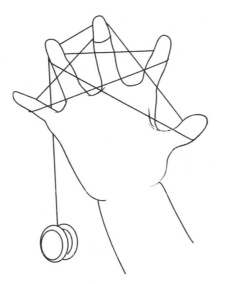

56.   Through the tunnel yo-yo trick

A variation on walk the dog, this advanced yo-yo trick sends the pooch through a tunnel.

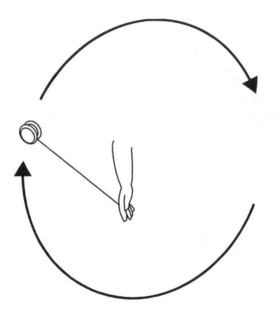

57.   Rattlesnake yo-yo trick

You can make your yo-yo move and sound like a rattlesnake in this amazing and fun yo-yo trick.

58. Shoot the moon yo-yo trick

This yo-yo trick can be dangerous, so practice with caution! When done correctly, the results are spectacular.

59. Elephant Trunk yo-yo Trick

You need to sound like an elephant to perform this fun advanced yo-yo trick.

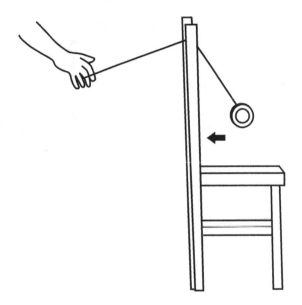

60.   Skyrocket yo-yo trick

Do you know you can send your yo-yo to the outer space? Yes, the other planets. The Skyrocket Yo-Yo Trick is a great addition to your yo-yo skills.

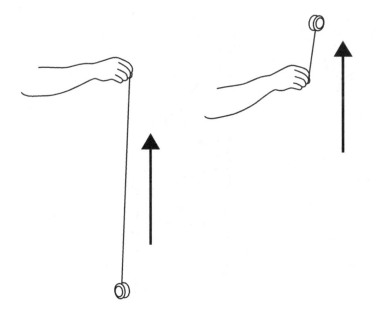

61. The man on the flying trapeze yo-yo trick

Thrill your family, friends, and classmates with this show-stopper YoYo trick. Learn one of the most difficult yo-yo tricks.

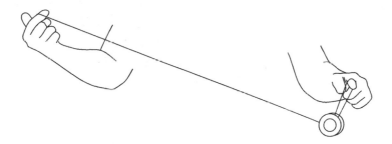

62. Double or nothing yo-yo trick

The double or nothing yoyo trick is actually very easy and fun to do.

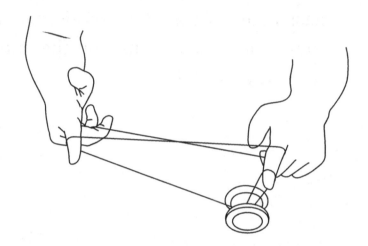

63. Bank deposit yo-yo trick

This unique yo-yo trick is a perfect finish to your yo-yo show. End your act on a high note with this fun and easy yoyo display.

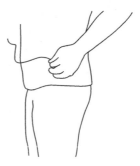

64.   **Rebound yoyo trick** - This
trick is pretty simple. Start by
bouncing the yoyo on the floor
of kicking it lightly.

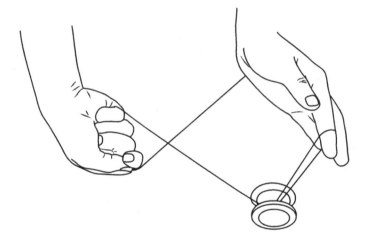

65. **Keychain yoyo trick** - The keychain yoyo trick otherwise known as the one finger spin yoyo trick is a nice trick to add to your list of routines.

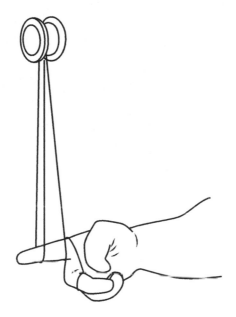

66.   Cross capture yoyo trick -
This is a cool trick and you do so
many variations of the trick. You
can do the up and down motion
and you can do the cross capture
with your arms crossed.

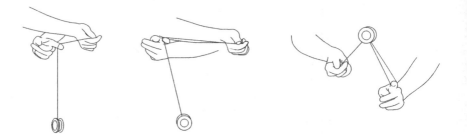

67.   Keymaker whip yoyo

trick - The Keymaker yoyo trick is a fun and cool trick that can be integrated into side mounts in different ways.

68.   Iron whip yoyo trick -
The iron whip yoyo trick is similar to jade whip. It's one of the tricks that requires you to have a strong string tension.

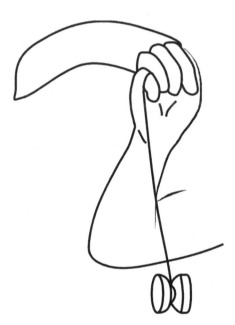

69. **Lord of the flies yoyo trick** - This is a mix of tricks put together. The trick starts with the iron whip trick and ends with the green triangle laceration.

70.   Serpentine yoyo trick -
This tricks starts with the
breakaway trick and ends with a
trapeze.

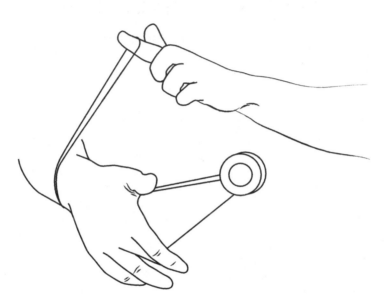

71. **Follow yoyo trick** - This trick is similar to jade whip except that you keep up with the motion of the yoyo, instead of keeping it fixed at a spot.

 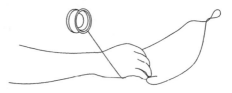

72.   Snap GT yoyo trick - The trick starts with a trapeze, followed by a trapeze and his brother trick.

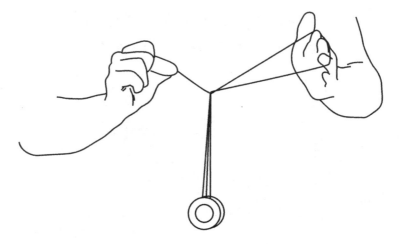

73.   Boomerang yoyo trick -

The boomerang yoyo trick is similar to a hop, except that you throw the hop right in front of you.

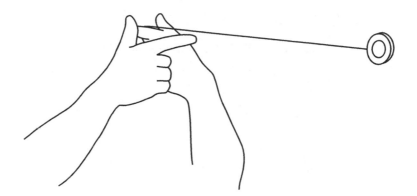

TRICKS

74. **Time warp yoyo trick** -
This trick is pretty simple. The
trick starts with Around the
World trick and ends with
reverse.

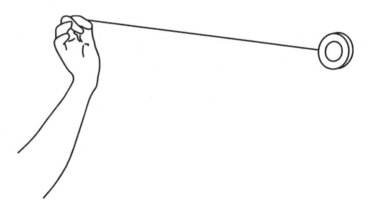

75. **Winder yoyo trick** - Spin
the yoyo with your free hand
and return to your throw hand.

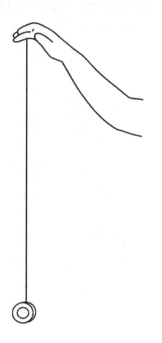

76. **Tower yoyo trick** - With the yoyo on the string, use the string to form the shape of a tower.

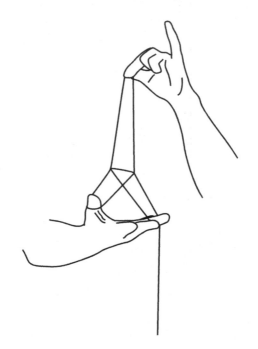

77.   Dizzy baby yoyo trick -
This trick starts with the rock the baby trick. Then spin the yoyotricks.com in circles like you do in pinwheel.

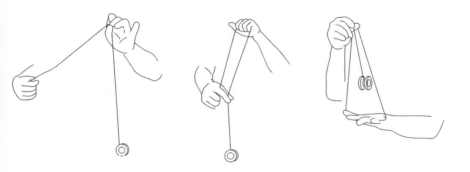

78.   Tidal wave yoyo trick -
This trick combines the sleeper
and the inside loop trick.

**79.   Sidethrow pinwheel yoyo
trick -** This trick requires you to
throw the yoyo right in front of
you and then swing it in circles.

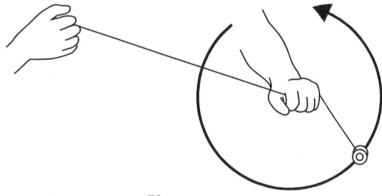

80. Throw down yoyo trick -
Throw the yoyo down and catch it with your palm facing down.

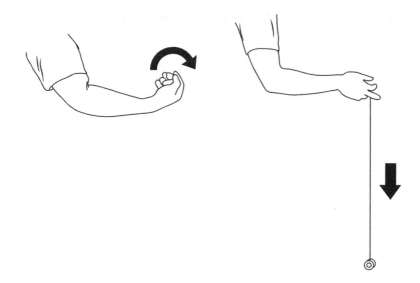

81. Side around the world sleeper yoyo trick – This trick

starts with the breakaway, then the sleeper and around the world trick.

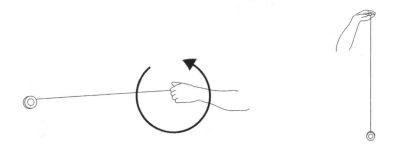

82.   Brain twister yoyo trick -

Attach the yoyo to the sting and flip it forward.

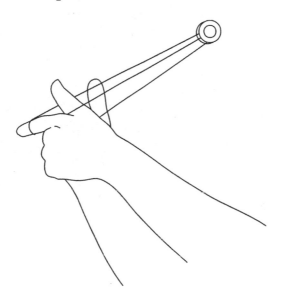

83. **Bind yoyo trick -** This trick starts with a sleeping trick, then return the yoyo by turning the string around it.

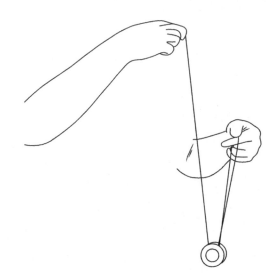

84. **Flying saucer yoyo trick -**
This trick requires you to place
your yoyo in a horizontal
position, then spin the string
above it and let it fall back to
your hand.

85.   Power sleeper yoyo trick
- The power sleeper trick gives your yoyo more power than the basic sleeper.

86.   Inside loop yoyo trick -
This trick starts with the sleeper
trick. Instead of catching the
yoyo when it comes back, rotate
your wrist and do a sleeper
again. Then catch it.

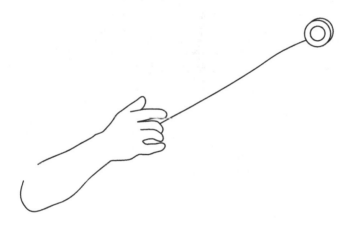

87.   **Elevator yoyo trick** - This trick is pretty simple. Simply slide the yoyo through the string like an elevator.

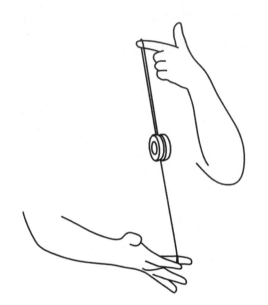

88.   Walk the dog yoyo trick - Start with a sleeper, then lower your yoyo slowly to the ground. Your yoyo will roll forward once it touches the ground. Then pick it up once it measures 30cm.

89.   Brain twister 2 yoyo trick

- This is an advanced version of
the brain twister trick.

90.   Planet hop yoyo trick -
Throw your yo-yo back and forth across your throw hand.

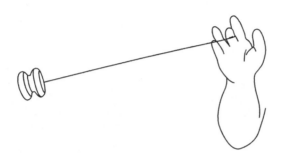

91.   Sidewinder yoyo trick -
Attach your yoyo to the string. Then throw it down and spin the string in coins as you catch the yoyo.

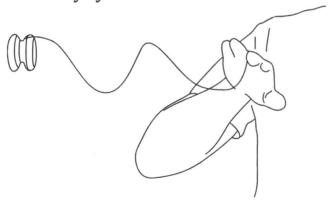

92. **Trapeze yoyo trick** - Start
with a break away. Then pop the
yoyo up with your forefinger
and catch.

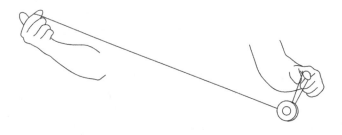

93.   Inside loop 10 yoyo trick

- Do 10 consecutive repetitions of inside loop without counting the first forward   pass.

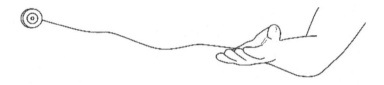

94.   Inside loop 3 yoyo trick - Do 3 repetitions of inside loop without counting the first forward pass.

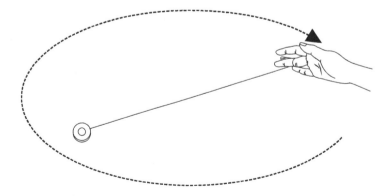

95.   Orbits/satellites

The yoyo orbits around a body part
such as the leg or waist.

96.   Knot/magic knot

The line is tangled so as to create the illusion that the yoyo is knotted. It can usually be released with an upward toss motion.

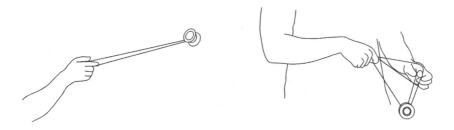

97.   Elevator/ladybug

The yoyo climbs up the string; this is done by wrapping the string around the axle and pulling tight.

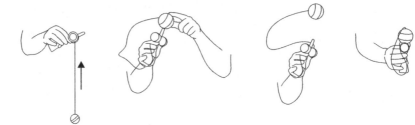

98.   Unresponsive   String Tension

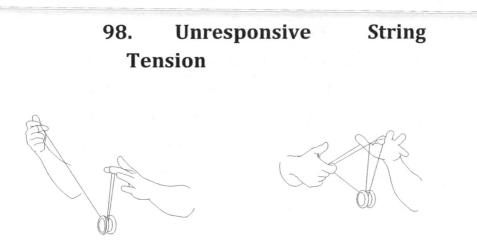

99.   Umbrella

The yoyo is swung and jerked side to side over both sticks, forming the outline of an umbrella.

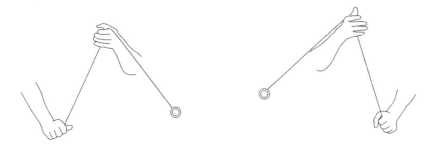

100. Files

You will put both sticks in the left hand, then swings the yoyo over your finger and back onto the string, so there is a trapeze-like tangle. Then throws the sticks under your finger and catches them again

101.   Steam engine

For this trick, you will need to pull the string down the side of the left stick and holds it with your left hand. Then you bring the right stick over the left and into the loop you've created. You'll then move the right stick in a small circle pushing at the loop. This will make the yoyo jump.

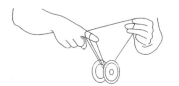 

ADVANCED TRICKS

There are countless tricks and variations that fall outside the above categories; these are often more difficult and form the cutting edge of modern yoyo routines. Some examples are:

102.   Genocide

Any trick in which the stick is released and the yoyo leaves the string. The yoyo is subsequently caught on the string again, and the stick is caught again.

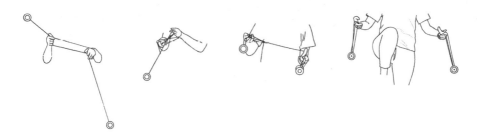

103. Whip catch

The yoyo is tossed into the air and caught with a whipping motion of the string towards the yoyo.

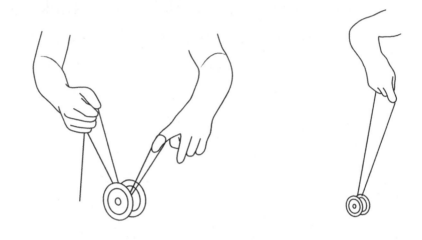

104. Finger grind

The spinning yoyo is balanced on a finger. This is best done with a bearing or triple bearing yoyo.

105. Infinite suicides

The yoyo appears to be suspended while one stick repeatedly orbits it, and the other stick travels in circles around the yoyo.

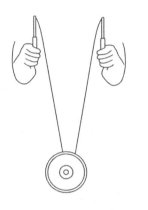

106.   Slack whips

The stick or sticks are flicked in such a way that a loop of slack in the string is made; this then passes around the yoyo and/or sticks to attain a range of different string mounts.

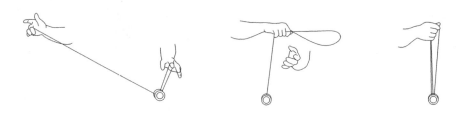

107.   Excalibur/vertical

A series of tricks in which the yoyo is turned vertical. Many tricks normally done outside of vertical can also be done in vertical.

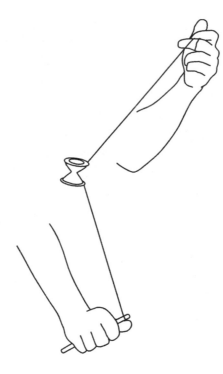

108. Integral

Any trick in which both sticks are released while the string is held.

109. Star Cradle

The strings are twisted into a star-shaped pattern.

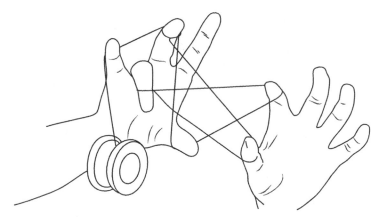

110.   Accelerations

The yoyos are accelerated while they wrap and the player's dominant hand is pulled up to gain speed. Doing a Chinese acceleration or shuffling the yoyos very quickly are two other methods of accelerating yoyos.

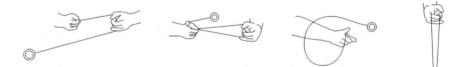

111. Hyperloop/sprinkler

The yoyos orbit each other inside a closed loop of string.

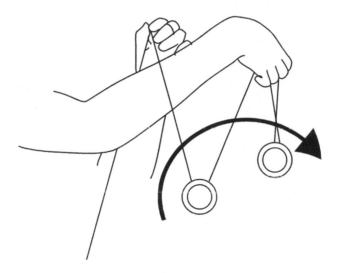

112. Columns/mini-columns

Two yoyos are bounced up and down on the string. Cascade and reverse cascade (also possible with juggling)

Three yoyos are bounced/thrown around in a cascade or reverse cascade pattern.

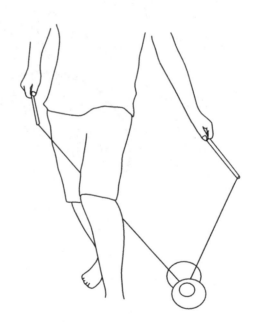

113. Siteswap

For this trick, the yoyos are thrown in different rhythms based on a numeric description. However, it's different from toss juggling as it uses a different system of numeric rhythms. For this trick, you can only use one "hand" as a string.

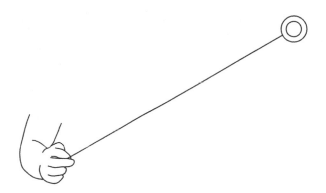

114.   Fan

Two yoyos are spun between the arms in a way which mimics the blades of a fan. While the yoyos rotate, they do not switch positions on the string.

115.   Sun

The yoyos are swung in a circle.

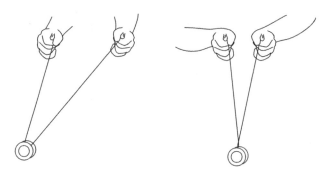

116.   Suicide

Multiple-yoyo suicides are similar to one-yoyo suicides, but some tricks are not possible.

117. Knots

Multiple-yoyo knots are similar to one-yoyo knots, but both yoyos are wrapped up.

118.   Stalls

This is where both yoyos are still spinning but not in shuffle. This allows the player to do a trick with the other.

119.   Contact yoyo

This is a relatively recent style of yoyo that is just gaining popularity. It utilizes the yo-yo only so that it has little or no spin at all. Then you can now try to catch it and pass it with different parts of the body instead of just the sticks and string.

120. Loop yoyo

Instead of the regular two sticks connected by a string, the yoyo is held on a loop of string held around the hands. This opens up a variety of new tricks such as suicides, suns, whips, stopovers, trapezes, two yoyos, and vertax.

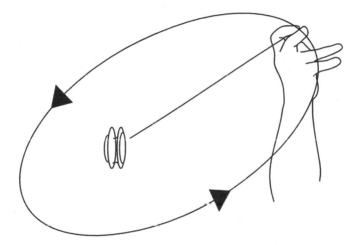

121. Guillotine yoyo trick

Bonus!

Would you like to have an exclusive article eBook that has **15 Top Quality Working on Crafts for Kids**?

http://bit.ly/2qWfaKT

Thank you for reading this book! I would like to give you full access to an exclusive article eBook that has **15 Top Quality Working on Crafts for Kids**. If you are someone who is interested in saving lots of money, then type in the website on your browser for **FREE** access!

Conclusion

Thank you again for downloading this book!

We hope this book helped with learning new yo-yo tricks and helps bring value to you! We hope you learn all the tricks you want and show off your skills.

Finally, if you enjoyed this book, then I'd like to ask you for a favor, would you be kind enough to leave a review for this book on amazon? I'd greatly appreciated!

Click here to leave a review for this book on Amazon!

Thank you and good luck!

Made in the USA
Las Vegas, NV
02 December 2021